Philosophy for children

From child to children

Once upon a time!

The donkey

From child to children

By: Bernardo Octaviano Pereira

This book belongs to:

____

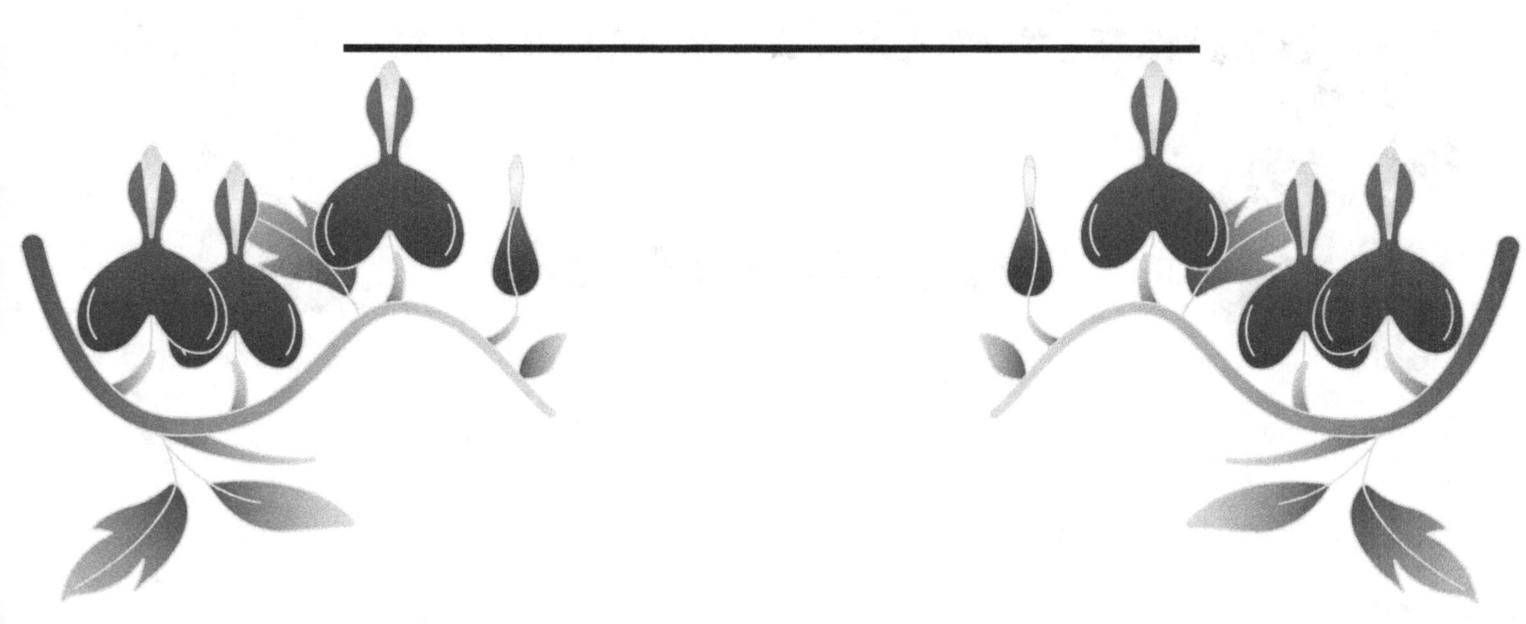

I dedicate this work, firstly, to my parents who I love so much, to my teachers, to my dear aunts and to all my friends, may God bless you all infinitely!

Bernardo Octaviano Pereira

02/04/2024

Once upon a time, on a farm not far from here, there lived a very bad farmer;

He didn't like anything or anyone, he was always mistreating people, employees and animals, and on that farm he had a donkey, which for the farmer only caused losses;

Who ate a lot and worked little, which the farmer wanted to get rid of anyway. One day the donkey was scared by a snake and ran wildly out of the playpen where she lived;

And he ran to where there was a little garden full of vegetables, stepping on everything that was in front of him, and destroying the little garden;

The farmer got very angry and ordered his employees to throw the donkey into the bottom of an old dry pit, which was no longer useful;

And with great sadness, even if they wanted to, the employees did, they will throw the donkey into the deep end;

The days went by, and the donkey remained alive at the bottom of the well, the days went by and to everyone's surprise, the donkey didn't die. Several days passed and the donkey didn't die, she didn't give up;

The farmer, irritated by the animal's persistence, instructed his employees to throw dirt into the pit to bury it alive.

And the employees who were initially reluctant to participate in the farmer's cruel order had to do it, very sadly, the employees were throwing dirt and the donkey was stepping on the earth and climbing on top of it, each layer of earth thrown into the well was responded to with the donkey's determination. to go up.

However, the donkey's fate took a surprising turn, determined not to surrender, the more dirt the employees threw, the donkey stepped on the ground and climbed on top of it, they started throwing it, stepping on it and climbing until it emerged victorious from the old well;

Instead of continuing with his cruel stance, the farmer, surprised by the lesson of resilience and overcoming, decided to free her, seeing the donkey's determination to want to live, and ordered the donkey to be released, which is still alive today and everyone was very happy on the farm.

The farm, once marked by sadness, was filled with joy. Everyone learned a valuable lesson about overcoming and the importance of not giving up in the face of challenges and finding strength in adversity.

The farmer began to see not only the animals, but also the people around him, in a different way.
May this story remind us of the strength of resilience and the capacity for transformation that we all have, regardless of the circumstances.

The end!

www.ingramcontent.com/pod-product-compliance
Lightning Source LLC
Chambersburg PA
CBHW081542250726
48659CB00009B/3045